Home Buying Guide

Chandler Crouch Realtors

ISBN: 1503130797
ISBN-13: 978-1503130791

817-381-3800
www.ChandlerCrouch.com
9500 Ray White Rd, 2nd Floor, Fort Worth, TX 76244

Table of Contents

Dear Client,

Thank you for giving us the opportunity to serve you.
Buying a home is one of the most important and exciting decisions of your life. It affects virtually every aspect of your family's life, either directly or indirectly.

Equal parts consultant, data analyst, and negotiator, your Chandler Crouch Realtors agent strives to make home buying more transparent and less stressful so you can focus on finding the house you love.

It is truly our pleasure to serve you.

Sincerely,

Chandler Crouch

CHANDLER CROUCH REALTORS
hello@chandlercrouch.com | 9500 Ray White Rd. 2nd Floor | (817) 381-3800

CHANDLER CROUCH REALTORS

Our company is different... From the founder to our management team to your personal Realtor, our **entire organization** is committed to the quality of your experience.

We work as a team. At our company you won't have the lone ranger Realtor attempt to do all the marketing, listing homes, accounting, administrative work, putting on lockboxes, office maintenance, and countless other tasks being stretched in 10 directions all while trying to help your family find their next home.

We've found when individuals specializing on specific tasks within their unique gifts and abilities, buyers have the best experience and results. After your Realtor help you find your new home and negotiates to get you the best deal, our transaction specialist will call you and begin working to ensure all deadlines are met and you receive the best communication every step of the way.

A family owned company founded in 2002 by Chandler and Meghan Crouch.
- 3 Highly Trained Staff, 6 Agents

Achievements
- Best of the Best in Keller – Keller Citizen Newspaper
- Wall Street Journal top 200 Realtors in America
- We have enjoyed working for Dave Ramsey, Glenn Beck, and the federal government
- Zillow & Trulia 5 star pro Realtor
- Featured on: Realtor.com, nar.com, entrepreneur.com, top rated iTunes podcasts

Memberships:
- Member of Asian Real Estate Association of America (AERAA)
- Member National Association of Hispanic Real Estate Professionals (NAHREP)
- Member of National Association of Real Estate Brokers (NAREB)
- Member of National Association of Broker Price Opinion Professionals (NABPOP)
- SFR—Short Sale and Foreclosure Resource Certified

Well Insured:
- Errors and Omissions Insurance, General/Commercial Liability, Commercial Automobile Liability, Coverage that includes fire, personal injury, medical, advertising

Other
- Certified education provider through the Texas Real Estate Commission

OUR APPROACH
SALESPERSON VS CONSULTANT

Our focus is on something much bigger than just this real estate transaction. We believe that trust is the most valuable thing we can earn in any transaction. So, instead of a high pressure sales approach, we are committed to a consultative approach to help you achieve your goals.

Our success is defined by your experience. We'll know we did our job if you feel compelled to **tell family and friends about your experience** and we earn **your business for life**.
Our goal at the end of this transaction is to earn a **5 star review**.

Our consultative approach is different...

- We work as a team
- We try to do business the way we feel business should be done... by doing the right thing
- Professional, methodical
- Invest time into preparation - assessing your needs
- Begin by securing financing & a prequalification letter
- Provide a list of homes, in real-time, that fit criteria YOU set

- Assist with any kind of home that fits your needs - builders, foreclosures, short sales, and for sale by owners
- Aggressively negotiate on your behalf to get you the best deal possible
- Our goals are to help you find a house:
    - At the price you want
    - In the time you choose
    - With the least amount of hassle

RENT VS. BUY

The benefits of buying instead of renting are too numerous to fit on this page. Here are 3 reasons that make buying vs renting a no-brainer:

Monthly savings

Stop Throwing Your Money Away
Rent VS Own for $3,000/month

	Rent	Buy
Loan Amount	N/A	$495,000
Interest Rate	N/A	4.125%
Total Payment	$3,000	$3,001.10
Tax Benefit	$0	$780.02
Principal Paid	$0	$697.46
Net Monthly Payment	$3,000	$1,523.62
Monthly Savings	$0	$1,476.33

$550k purchase price with 10% down, no PMI, 4.125% APR

No Annual Rent Increase

Buying is Cheaper in the Long Run
Annual rent increase: 4.9% (compounds annually)

Annual increase in a fix rate mortgage: $0

Source: Forbes.com

You Build Wealth
As Your Home Value Appreciates

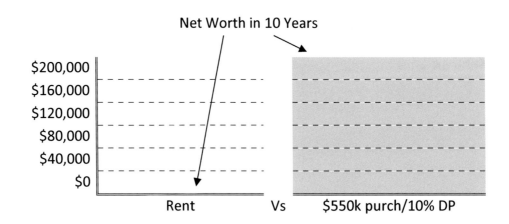

A GOOD TIME TO BUY?

Do you know the difference between a **buyer's market vs seller's market**?
Our current market is a seller's market so **sellers are getting to choose the price and terms they want** as buyers compete for houses, however our market is unique... It favors both buyers and sellers.
Here are 3 ways buyers benefit from our current market...

1. **Interest rates** are at a historic lows (but not forever). The amount of money you will save on mortgage interest is far greater than any meager discount you might have found in a buyer's market. For example, on a $300,000 house the difference in savings between a 4.5% interest rate vs a 6.5% interest rate is $132,288.61.*

    This chart shows how your purchasing power is affected when interest rates go up.

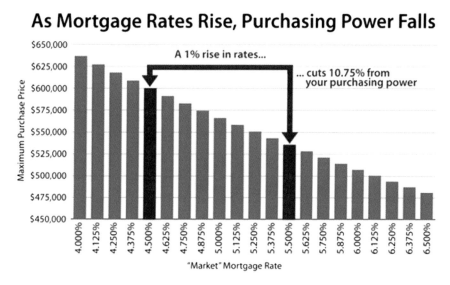

2. Sellers are motivated to make **quick decisions**. Sellers know buyers are being trained by the market and can't afford to wait long for the seller to respond to an offer.

3. You are buying into an **appreciating market**. This means even if you buy at 100% of market value now, tomorrow your purchase price will be less than market value. Appreciating assets cause wealth accumulation.

Discover why Forbes is saying Texas is the **best place in the country to invest** and get more market information here: www.chandlercrouch.com/market

*Side note: Ask how I can save you an additional $41,801.53

6 STEPS TO HOME OWNERSHIP

1. **6 Months or More Prior to Move-In**
   Select an Experienced Realtor. Discuss your timeline and needs

2. 6 Months or More Prior to Move-In
   Secure Financing. Get prequalified. Fix credit errors, prevent last minute costly delays (even a 1 hour delay making an offer can be costly).

3. 4-6 Months Prior to Move-In
   Refine Your Search. This is your homework. Determine needs vs wants. Research, visit neighborhoods at different times of the day. Map out shopping and schools.

4. 2-3 Months Prior to Move-In
   Select a Home. View houses.
   NAR reports 10 houses are viewed on average.
   We show you the best houses first. Up to 5 houses per outing.
   It's not uncommon for the very first house you see to be the one you want to purchase.
   Schedule showings 24 hours in advance. Place an offer.

5. 30-45 Days Prior to Move-In
   The Transaction Process. Secure financing, home inspection, appraisal, approval through underwriting (more details on the next page)

6. 30-45 days after getting your offer accepted
   Move Into Your New Home! Schedule the move, activate utilities, final walk through, closing.

SELECT AN EXPERT REALTOR
HISTORY OF BUYER AGENCY

- A history of buyer agency: **Buyer agency began in the 90's** after the FTC released a report that would change the industry. The report indicated that 72% of home buyers believed that the real estate agent working *with* them was working *for* them. This was in direct contradiction to the reality of business practices at the time in which all licensees either worked for the sellers as listing agents or for the seller as sub-agents to the listing agents while working with the buyers. In 1993 a class action lawsuit awarded $200 million dollars in damages. The law suit marked the turning point for buyers. Buyer agency was born and now buyers that choose to have representation now enjoy the benefits of being treated as an equal in the transaction.

- The government says we should operate with a written agreement, and it's the right way to do business. **We provide buyer agency to 100% of our buyer clients**.

- **Realtors are able to find out more information** than what is publically available.

- **Calling me first** will allow me to answer you in a **paragraph rather than a sentence**. As your representative, I am duty bound to find out and tell you as much information as I can. If I know what the seller's motivating factors are, such as a divorce or relocation, as a Buyer's Agent I will tell you, therefore increasing your leverage in negotiations. As a sub-agent to the seller or an intermediary (transactional broker), I can't tell you anything.

SELECT AN EXPERT REALTOR
BUYER AGENCY

Information About Brokerage Services

Texas law requires all real estate license holders to give the following information about brokerage services to prospective buyers, tenants, sellers and landlords.

11-2-2015

TYPES OF REAL ESTATE LICENSE HOLDERS:
- **A BROKER** is responsible for all brokerage activities, including acts performed by sales agents sponsored by the broker.
- **A SALES AGENT** must be sponsored by a broker and works with clients on behalf of the broker.

A BROKER'S MINIMUM DUTIES REQUIRED BY LAW (A client is the person or party that the broker represents):
- Put the interests of the client above all others, including the broker's own interests;
- Inform the client of any material information about the property or transaction received by the broker;
- Answer the client's questions and present any offer to or counter-offer from the client; and
- Treat all parties to a real estate transaction honestly and fairly.

A LICENSE HOLDER CAN REPRESENT A PARTY IN A REAL ESTATE TRANSACTION:

AS AGENT FOR OWNER (SELLER/LANDLORD): The broker becomes the property owner's agent through an agreement with the owner, usually in a written listing to sell or property management agreement. An owner's agent must perform the broker's minimum duties above and must inform the owner of any material information about the property or transaction known by the agent, including information disclosed to the agent or subagent by the buyer or buyer's agent.

AS AGENT FOR BUYER/TENANT: The broker becomes the buyer/tenant's agent by agreeing to represent the buyer, usually through a written representation agreement. A buyer's agent must perform the broker's minimum duties above and must inform the buyer of any material information about the property or transaction known by the agent, including information disclosed to the agent by the seller or seller's agent.

AS AGENT FOR BOTH - INTERMEDIARY: To act as an intermediary between the parties the broker must first obtain the written agreement of *each party* to the transaction. The written agreement must state who will pay the broker and, in conspicuous bold or underlined print, set forth the broker's obligations as an intermediary. A broker who acts as an intermediary:
- Must treat all parties to the transaction impartially and fairly;
- May, with the parties' written consent, appoint a different license holder associated with the broker to each party (owner and buyer) to communicate with, provide opinions and advice to, and carry out the instructions of each party to the transaction.
- Must not, unless specifically authorized in writing to do so by the party, disclose:
  - o that the owner will accept a price less than the written asking price;
  - o that the buyer/tenant will pay a price greater than the price submitted in a written offer; and
  - o any confidential information or any other information that a party specifically instructs the broker in writing not to disclose, unless required to do so by law.

AS SUBAGENT: A license holder acts as a subagent when aiding a buyer in a transaction without an agreement to represent the buyer. A subagent can assist the buyer but does not represent the buyer and must place the interests of the owner first.

TO AVOID DISPUTES, ALL AGREEMENTS BETWEEN YOU AND A BROKER SHOULD BE IN WRITING AND CLEARLY ESTABLISH:
- The broker's duties and responsibilities to you, and your obligations under the representation agreement.
- Who will pay the broker for services provided to you, when payment will be made and how the payment will be calculated.

LICENSE HOLDER CONTACT INFORMATION: This notice is being provided for information purposes. It does not create an obligation for you to use the broker's services. Please acknowledge receipt of this notice below and retain a copy for your records.

6 Steps to Home Ownership

1. 6 Months or More Prior to Move-In
   Select an Experienced Realtor. Discuss your timeline and needs

2. 6 Months or More Prior to Move-In
   Secure Financing. Get prequalified. Fix credit errors, prevent last minute costly delays (even a 1 hour delay making an offer can be costly).

3. 4-6 Months Prior to Move-In
   Refine Your Search. This is your homework. Determine needs vs wants. Research, visit neighborhoods at different times of the day. Map out shopping and schools.

4. 2-3 Months Prior to Move-In
   Select a Home. View houses.
   NAR reports 10 houses are viewed on average.
   We show you the best houses first. Up to 5 houses per outing.
   It's not uncommon for the very first house you see to be the one you want to purchase.
   Schedule showings 24 hours in advance. Place an offer.

5. 30-45 Days Prior to Move-In
   The Transaction Process. Secure financing, home inspection, appraisal, approval through underwriting (more details on the next page)

6. 30-45 days after getting your offer accepted
   Move Into Your New Home! Schedule the move, activate utilities, final walk through, closing.

SECURE FINANCING
HOW TO SELECT A LENDER

The success of your transaction depends on the quality of your lender.

Mortgage lending is becoming more complex every day. Political maneuvering, onerous regulations, and daily changes in lending requirements make it more important than ever to work with a reputable mortgage lender. To identify a quality lender, follow these 2 simple steps:

1. Work with a lender that is referred by an industry expert. We don't receive compensation (kickbacks) for referring any lender. We only refer someone if we feel like they are truly the best person to serve you, not for any other reason.
   a. If someone we refer you to does a bad job, they could lose our business, which would be costly.
   b. We have insight that can only be obtained through experience to help us identify sub-par practitioners.

2. Lenders notoriously promise more than they can deliver. Please shop around until you find a lender you feel confident about. All we ask is that **if you choose a lender outside of our referral network you screen the lender by using the 5 questions on the next page**.
   If you would like help interviewing a lender, just let us know. We are happy to help.

SECURE FINANCING
5 QUESTIONS TO IDENTIFY AN EXCEPTIONAL LENDER

1. What happens to our timeline if the rate goes up 1/8 of a percent?
    a. This requires the lender to send you an updated estimate for your review. Depending on the lender's process this will cause a closing delay of 3 to 6 days. You want a lender that guarantees their fees.
2. What is the minimum information I can give you to get an <u>official</u> good faith estimate (GFE)?
    a. Address, Loan Amount, Income, Estimated Value, Name, and Social Security Number. Without an official GFE, the lender is free to change fees and rate. Unofficial estimates are great for general info, but knowing when the estimate is an official GFE protects you.
3. Is there a maximum amount of fee increase that can take place from your estimate to closing?
    a. Answer, YES & NO. Your lender will provide an estimate of their own fees and also some 3rd party fees (eg appraisal fee). The estimate for the lender's own fees cannot change by 1 cent. 3rd party fees can change by up to 10%. Watch out for lenders offering low 3rd party estimates.
4. How does your company handle the 3 day waiting period before I can close?
    a. Some lenders will have you electronically sign the closing statement the same day it is prepared so that you can close 3 days later. This is the fastest way to closing. Other lenders will "mail" the closing statement which will force the buyer to wait 6 days as opposed to 3 days. This can make or break a deal at the last minute.
5. Does your company have a recast policy?
    a. Recasting is the cheapest way to refinance. If you want to make a large cash payment on your mortgage you can recast to lower your monthly payment. Not recasting option will cause your payment will remain at the same level no matter how much you pay off.

SECURE FINANCING
HOW DOES PREQUALIFICATION AFFECT MY CREDIT SCORE?

Getting prequalified can take as little as 10 minutes.

There are a few specific reasons why getting prequalified for a mortgage leaves your credit **virtually unscathed**. Some people are surprised to hear getting prequalified may actually help **improve** their credit score.

The Better Business Bureau found that **42 million Americans** have errors on their credit report. Getting prequalified in advance will help you identify and fix errors which could lead to a lower interest rate and significant savings.

On top of it being a good idea, most sellers won't even consider an offer unless it is accompanied by a prequalification letter.

How Credit Bureau Scoring Works

Did you know that when a car dealer (or another kind of lender) pulls your credit the score they see a different score than when a mortgage lender pulls your credit? Each industry has its own unique algorithm of calculating your credit score.

For instance, mortgage lenders have found that responsible borrowers will accumulate multiple mortgage related credit inquiries immediately preceding their home purchase.

Consequently, the credit scoring system now allows for multiple mortgage related credit inquires to be lumped together and counted as only 1 inquiry affecting a borrowers credit score at a level of only **1-3 points** – a negligible amount especially if you consider the accompanying benefits.

Our preferred lender provides a quick and easy 10 minute express application that you can complete using estimated figures: www.chandlercrouch.com/app

SECURE FINANCING
BEYOND PRE-QUALIFICATION

After you get prequalified, **immediately begin preparing and delivering these documents to the lender** to complete the approval process:

Employment Information:
- Employer information for the past 2 years
    - Company name, address, and contact information.
    - Explanation and documentation for any gap of employment during 2 year history.
- Year to date pay stubs
- Last 2 years' W-2s.
- Diploma or transcript if you were a student during the past 2 years

Other Income Documentation:
- Self-employed business income: profit and loss statement
- Rental Income: Copy of lease which is current and at least one year in length.
- Alimony and Child Support (only if used for qualification): Copy of divorce decree and property settlement (ratified) settling out terms. Proof of payment will also be requested at application.
- Income From Notes Held: A copy of ratified note.
- Retirement, Social Security and Disability Income: Copy of award letter and latest check showing amount of present payment. Copy of end of year statement if applicable.

Assets:
- Bank Accounts: Name of bank, address, account numbers, types of accounts, present balances on savings accounts, and average balances on checking accounts.
- Copy of two most recent statements of all accounts.
- Stocks and Bonds: Copy of certificates or copy of recent (within 30 days) broker statement listing the holdings.
- Life Insurance: Cash value, only if being used for down payment.
- Vehicles: Year, make, and value. Copy of title is under 4 years old with no outstanding lien.
- Real Estate: Address and market value. If free and clear, deed of release, deed or mortgage payoff.
- Present Home: Copy of sales contract, settlement sheet and/or lease.
- Gift Letter: Form will be provided by financial representative. Donor Capacity must be verified. Receipt of funds must be shown in account.

Additional documentation may be necessary for VA or other types of loans

SECURE FINANCING
DO'S & DON'TS

The following Do's and Don'ts are necessary to ensure a successful transaction. Not following these could result in hurt negotiations, **the deal not closing, and possibly even forfeiture of your earnest money**. It's important to begin following these from now until your loan is funded. Credit, income, and assets may be verified the hour before closing.

- **DO sign and return all documents** the lender sends you ASAP (ideally within 4 hours).
- **DO return phone calls** from your agent, loan officer, title company or anyone else involved in your transaction ASAP (ideally within 2 hours).
- **DO** make all payments on or before due dates on all accounts, even if the account is being paid off with your new loan. This includes mortgages, car loans, credit cards, etc.
- **DO** keep copies of all pay stubs, bank statements, and other important financial documentation that you receive before closing.
- **DO** keep documentation ("paper trail") on any large deposits into your account: copies of all paperwork necessary to prove a financial transaction, including all checks, deposit slips, loan paperwork, forms to liquidate assets, etc.

- **DO** obtain homeowner's insurance with minimum coverage equal to the amount of your total loan or the replacement value of the house.
- **DO** inform us if your address changes from what appears on our original loan application.
- **DO** notify us if your salary or other compensation changes from what appears on your original loan application.
- **DON'T** wait until you have 100% of your documentation (ie bank statements, paycheck stubs etc) before delivering them to the lender. **If you only have 50%, go ahead and send the documents you have so the lender can begin working**.
- **DON'T** quit or change jobs. If this is likely, consult with your loan officer and Realtor.
- **DON'T** allow anyone to make an inquiry on your credit or apply for credit anywhere except with your mortgage lender.
- **DON'T** attempt to purchase anything on credit such as another car, boat, furniture, appliances, carpet, or **home improvement items**.

- **DON'T** change bank accounts or transfer money within your existing accounts. If it is unavoidable, discuss it with your loan officer in advance and keep all documentation to provide a paper trail.
- **DON'T** co-sign for anyone for any reason for anything.
- **DON'T** charge any abnormal amounts to your current credit cards or credit lines.

6 STEPS TO HOME OWNERSHIP

1. 6 Months or More Prior to Move-In
   Select an Experienced Realtor. Discuss your timeline and needs

2. 6 Months or More Prior to Move-In
   Secure Financing. Get prequalified. Fix credit errors, prevent last minute costly delays (even a 1 hour delay making an offer can be costly).

3. 4-6 Months Prior to Move-In
   Refine Your Search. This is your homework. Determine needs vs wants. Research, visit neighborhoods at different times of the day. Map out shopping and schools.

4. 2-3 Months Prior to Move-In
   Select a Home. View houses.
   NAR reports 10 houses are viewed on average.
   We show you the best houses first. Up to 5 houses per outing.
   It's not uncommon for the very first house you see to be the one you want to purchase.
   Schedule showings 24 hours in advance. Place an offer.

5. 30-45 Days Prior to Move-In
   The Transaction Process. Secure financing, home inspection, appraisal, approval through underwriting (more details on the next page)

6. 30-45 days after getting your offer accepted
   Move Into Your New Home! Schedule the move, activate utilities, final walk through, closing.

REFINE YOUR SEARCH
BUYER PLAN OF ACTION

Did you know that Zillow, Trulia, and most other publically accessible websites get their information from the same source? That source is the Realtor exclusive Multiple Listing Service (MLS). The MLS is the gold standard of accurate property listing information. This is the source of data that every appraiser uses when gathering information for an appraisal, and it is highly regulated by the Board of Realtors through funding provided by Realtors expensive membership dues.

Public websites are decent at providing general historical market data, however, because these sites are not the originating source of the listing information provided on their website, there are often times a major delays in the data

transferring from the MLS to Zillow (and the other public sites). To make matters worse, unlike the MLS, the public site's primary objective is not to maintain accurate information. It is to generate leads of potential buyers so they can sell the leads to Realtors. These websites are able to generate many more leads by allowing recently sold listings to deceptively appear as active and still on the market long after the status of the property has changed.

These factors result in a **massive amount of inaccurate and outdated information**, which makes it a very poor source for a buyer to rely on when the time comes for the buyer to actually find a home to purchase.

Chandler Crouch Realtors is a Premier 5 Star Zillow agent and Trulia Pro agent. We know first-hand how to best utilize (and when not to utilize) these public sites to benefit our clients. For accurate real time property information, allow us to help.

REFINE YOUR SEARCH
TYPES OF HOMES & WHAT TO DO

As you begin your search, you may encounter various types of homes. Each type have unique negotiating styles, pricing strategies, and timeframes that must be considered.

When you find a home you are interested in, no matter the type, take the following action:

1. Call your Realtor first
2. Take a photo of the sign or address of the property
3. Text or email your Realtor the property information

Traditional (Resale) Homes – These are 90% of the homes you'll see. Anytime you see a house with a Realtor's sign in the front yard, it is likely a traditional home. The good news is that **all brokers have access to the same information**. I mention this because I've had clients in the past that didn't understand that **I can show them any listing** out there. So if the home is listed by another company, I can show you that home, represent your best interests and the best part is that the seller pays all my fees.

Builder Homes – Have you ever heard of the **85% principle**? People may light heartedly say they found the "perfect" home, but in reality **no home can be 100% perfect – in condition or in meeting 100% of your wish list items.** Most people feel excited about moving forward when a home meets about 85% of their wish list criteria. The only way to reliably get above the 85% threshold is to build the house exactly the way you want it. You still won't get to 100%, but you'll get a lot closer. If 85% doesn't seem reasonable to you, you may be a candidate for a builder home. Keep in mind, new construction takes on average 7 months to complete.

What should you do if you see a builder home and want to take a look? The best first step is always to **call your Realtor**. Studies have shown that buyers end up getting a better deal on new construction when they have representation.

Would you like every salesperson in North Texas calling you? Of course not. If you just can't wait to coordinate schedules with your Realtor, you must hand one of your Realtor's business cards to the builder sales associate as soon as you walk in the model home. If proper notice isn't given, the builder representative may force you to go through the transaction unrepresented. Handing them the Realtor's business card will also ensure that they call and hound your Realtor instead of you.

For Sale By Owner (FSBO) – If you see a FSBO that you would like to get more information about, give your Realtor a call. **Realtors have more information** about real estate than what is publically available. Your Realtor is also a more economic option to completing the contract. **Attorneys bill by the hour.** If you begin contract negotiations and the attorney has to put in extra work, the any advantage you gain in negotiations may be offset by extra time spent on the negotiations by the attorney. Also, if there are any disputes or worse, **if the deal falls apart, the attorney**  **will still demand their fees**. A Realtor only gets paid if you get the home, and **we negotiate for the seller to pay all commissions**.

Short Sales - These are sellers who owe more than what they can sell their home for and therefore have to negotiate with their bank to receive a lesser amount. Typically, the negotiation process with the bank can take 4-6 months to get an offer approved and the price is subject to change during this time. There is also a chance that the bank will reject the seller's request for a short sale and instead foreclose on it. Our company is accustomed to assisting buyers and sellers on short sale transactions. In most cases, it is to the buyer's advantage to **only consider short sales that have been approved by the lender** due to the unpredictable nature of a home in the preliminary stages of a short sale, that has yet to be approved by the lender.

Foreclosures—These are homes which have been foreclosed on and taken back by the bank, also known as REO's (Real Estate Owned) or "bank owned". Banks are motivated to sell these homes quickly and will typically price them slightly below market value to get multiple offers. Even though you may pay over the asking price, these can still be great values. Our company has a team that specifically works with foreclosures. We have unique insight that our buyers are sure to benefit from.

6 Steps to Home Ownership

1. 6 Months or More Prior to Move-In
   Select an Experienced Realtor. Discuss your timeline and needs

2. 6 Months or More Prior to Move-In
   Secure Financing. Get prequalified. Fix credit errors, prevent last minute costly delays (even a 1 hour delay making an offer can be costly).

3. 4-6 Months Prior to Move-In
   Refine Your Search. This is your homework. Determine needs vs wants. Research, visit neighborhoods at different times of the day. Map out shopping and schools.

4. 2-3 Months Prior to Move-In
   Select a Home. View houses.
   NAR reports 10 houses are viewed on average.
   We show you the best houses first. Up to 5 houses per outing.
   It's not uncommon for the very first house you see to be the one you want to purchase.
   Schedule showings 24 hours in advance. Place an offer.

5. 30-45 Days Prior to Move-In
   The Transaction Process. Secure financing, home inspection, appraisal, approval through underwriting (more details on the next page)

6. 30-45 days after getting your offer accepted
   Move Into Your New Home! Schedule the move, activate utilities, final walk through, closing.

SELECT A HOME
BUYER PLAN OF ACTION

In this market, it takes a proactive and aggressive approach to find you the best home at the best price. If we can't find your home available on the open market, we will exhaust other resources.

Off Market Properties—We are constantly marketing to find sellers before they list their home on the market. If we can identify a home that fits your criteria before it is listed on the market, you will be the first to know about it allowing you to get a jump on the competition.

Expired, Cancelled, Withdrawn, Pending Listings—We don't just search the "Active" properties on the MLS, we also search houses that are under contract or off the market. Not long ago one of our Realtors was assertive in finding out that a pending listing was about to come back out on the market. Our client was able to get an offer in before it was listed on the open market to secure the deal.

Database—We have a database of over 3,000 past, current and prospective clients who we actively communicate with. We often have home owners that would love to sell their house without the hassle of preparing their home to go on the market. This is another source of homes we will tap into for your benefit.

6 STEPS TO HOME OWNERSHIP

1. 6 Months or More Prior to Move-In
   Select an Experienced Realtor. Discuss your timeline and needs

2. 6 Months or More Prior to Move-In
   Secure Financing. Get prequalified. Fix credit errors, prevent last minute costly delays (even a 1 hour delay making an offer can be costly).

3. 4-6 Months Prior to Move-In
   Refine Your Search. This is your homework. Determine needs vs wants. Research, visit neighborhoods at different times of the day. Map out shopping and schools.

4. 2-3 Months Prior to Move-In
   Select a Home. View houses.
   NAR reports 10 houses are viewed on average.
   We show you the best houses first. Up to 5 houses per outing.
   It's not uncommon for the very first house you see to be the one you want to purchase.
   Schedule showings 24 hours in advance. Place an offer.

5. 30-45 Days Prior to Move-In
   The Transaction Process. Secure financing, home inspection, appraisal, approval through underwriting (more details on the next page)

6. 30-45 days after getting your offer accepted
   Move Into Your New Home! Schedule the move, activate utilities, final walk through, closing.

THE TRANSACTION
PREPARATION TO NEGOTIATIONS

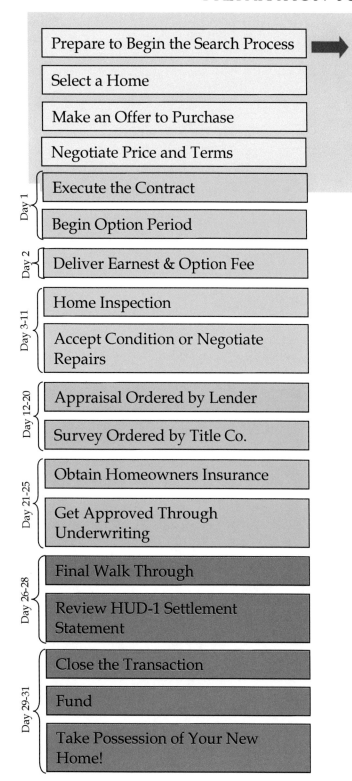

Prepare to Begin the Search Process →

Select a Home

Make an Offer to Purchase

Negotiate Price and Terms

Day 1 {
Execute the Contract

Begin Option Period

Day 2 {
Deliver Earnest & Option Fee

Day 3-11 {
Home Inspection

Accept Condition or Negotiate Repairs

Day 12-20 {
Appraisal Ordered by Lender

Survey Ordered by Title Co.

Day 21-25 {
Obtain Homeowners Insurance

Get Approved Through Underwriting

Day 26-28 {
Final Walk Through

Review HUD-1 Settlement Statement

Day 29-31 {
Close the Transaction

Fund

Take Possession of Your New Home!

Prepare Earnest & Option Fee

Pre-Qualification & Pre-Approval

Proof of Funds

Letter from the Buyer

THE TRANSACTION
MAKING AN OFFER

It's very important for you to **be comfortable with this contract. When we find the right home, moving forward without hesitation will prevent you from missing out** on the house you fall in love with.

First, allow me to explain what an offer is.

To make an offer, we fill out the contract according to the price and terms of your choosing then deliver it to the seller. If the seller signs the contract, we have an accepted offer. If the seller doesn't agree to the terms you suggested, he can strike through any undesirable terms and propose new terms. This is called a counter offer. We continue in this back and forth until all terms are agreed upon. This back and forth process is part of negotiating. The average person in **our culture has a low tolerance for negotiating**. Most want to reach a conclusion quickly and move on.

About this contract:

This contract was **drafted by the governmental department** called the Texas Real Estate Commission. The contract was written to clarify the agreement being made between buyer and seller and not designed to favor one party or the other. The data written in the **blanks is what will determine whether the contract favors the buyer or seller**.

Understanding each paragraph:

With your permission, your **Realtor will discuss the blanks of the contract that most affect your pocket book and timeline**. A full 2 hour explanation of each paragraph can be found on our website at www.chandlercrouch.com/contract

THE TRANSACTION

PROMULGATED BY THE TEXAS REAL ESTATE COMMISSION (TREC)
ONE TO FOUR FAMILY RESIDENTIAL CONTRACT (RESALE)
NOTICE: Not For Use For Condominium Transactions

11-2-2015

1. PARTIES: The parties to this contract are _____
(Seller) and _____ (Buyer).
Seller agrees to sell and convey to Buyer and Buyer agrees to buy from Seller the Property defined below.

2. PROPERTY: The land, improvements and accessories are collectively referred to as the "Property".
  A. LAND: Lot _____ Block _____, _____
      Addition, City of _____ , County of _____,
      Texas, known as _____
      (address/zip code), or as described on attached exhibit.
  B. IMPROVEMENTS: The house, garage and all other fixtures and improvements attached to the above-described real property, including without limitation, the following **permanently installed and built-in items,** if any: all equipment and appliances, valances, screens, shutters, awnings, wall-to-wall carpeting, mirrors, ceiling fans, attic fans, mail boxes, television antennas, mounts and brackets for televisions and speakers, heating and air-conditioning units, security and fire detection equipment, wiring, plumbing and lighting fixtures, chandeliers, water softener system, kitchen equipment, garage door openers, cleaning equipment, shrubbery, landscaping, outdoor cooking equipment, and all other property owned by Seller and attached to the above described real property.
  C. ACCESSORIES: The following described related accessories, if any: window air conditioning units, stove, fireplace screens, curtains and rods, blinds, window shades, draperies and rods, door keys, mailbox keys, above ground pool, swimming pool equipment and maintenance accessories, artificial fireplace logs, and controls for: (i) garage doors, (ii) entry gates, and (iii) other improvements and accessories.
  D. EXCLUSIONS: The following improvements and accessories will be retained by Seller and must be removed prior to delivery of possession: _____
      _____.

3. SALES PRICE:
  A. Cash portion of Sales Price payable by Buyer at closing .... $ _____
  B. Sum of all financing described in the attached: ☐ Third Party Financing Addendum,
    ☐ Loan Assumption Addendum, ☐ Seller Financing Addendum .... $ _____
  C. Sales Price (Sum of A and B) .... $ _____

4. LICENSE HOLDER DISCLOSURE: Texas law requires a real estate license holder who is a party to a transaction or acting on behalf of a spouse, parent, child, business entity in which the license holder owns more than 10%, or a trust for which the license holder acts as a trustee or of which the license holder or the license holder's spouse, parent or child is a beneficiary, to notify the other party in writing before entering into a contract of sale. Disclose if applicable: _____
_____

5. EARNEST MONEY: Upon execution of this contract by all parties, Buyer shall deposit
$ _____ s earnest money with _____, as escrow agent,
at _____ (address). Buyer shall deposit additional earnest money of $ _____ with escrow agent within _____ days after the effective date of this contract. If Buyer fails to deposit the earnest money as required by this contract, Buyer will be in default.

6. TITLE POLICY AND SURVEY:
  A. TITLE POLICY: Seller shall furnish to Buyer at ☐ Seller's ☐ Buyer's expense an owner policy of title insurance (Title Policy) issued by _____ (Title Company) in the amount of the Sales Price, dated at or after closing, insuring Buyer against loss under the provisions of the Title Policy, subject to the promulgated exclusions (including existing building and zoning ordinances) and the following exceptions:
    (1) Restrictive covenants common to the platted subdivision in which the Property is located.
    (2) The standard printed exception for standby fees, taxes and assessments.
    (3) Liens created as part of the financing described in Paragraph 3.
    (4) Utility easements created by the dedication deed or plat of the subdivision in which the Property is located.

THE TRANSACTION

Paragraph 3 is where we write the sales price.

The first blank is the down payment, the second blank is the amount you are financing, and the third blank is the total purchase price (blanks 1 and 2 added together).

How much should you offer? That's up to you.

Since **your goal is to purchase** the home, it's smart to make sure you're offering something that is within a range that the seller will consider. There is no need for guess work here. We will look to see what the actual **list price to sales price ratio** is for the specific market you are interested in so that you are armed with the facts.

One thing to consider. For the typical north texas home, **for every $1000 you add to your purchase price, it will increase your monthly payment $6-$8**.

Paragraph 5 is for your earnest money deposit. This is the money you deposit with the title company (an unbiased third party) to show the seller that you are serious about wanting to buy the property. The **seller is expecting at least 1%**, although you can deposit any amount you choose. **The more money you deposit the more serious your offer will appear**. To gain additional leverage in the negotiations, it is not uncommon to deposit as much as 2%-10%. This money will be protected by paragraph 4 and paragraph 23. **This money is not a fee**. It will be credited to you at closing.

Paragraph 6 is designed to protect you as well. This is what insures that you are purchasing a property free and clear of any liens or back taxes etc. We will negotiate for the seller to pay for this insurance.

THE TRANSACTION

(5) Reservations or exceptions otherwise permitted by this contract or as may be approved by Buyer in writing.

(6) The standard printed exception as to marital rights.

(7) The standard printed exception as to waters, tidelands, beaches, streams, and related matters.

(8) The standard printed exception as to discrepancies, conflicts, shortages in area or boundary lines, encroachments or protrusions, or overlapping improvements: ☐(i) will not be amended or deleted from the title policy; or ☐(ii) will be amended to read, "shortages in area" at the expense of ☐Buyer ☐Seller.

B. COMMITMENT: Within 20 days after the Title Company receives a copy of this contract, Seller shall furnish to Buyer a commitment for title insurance (Commitment) and, at Buyer's expense, legible copies of restrictive covenants and documents evidencing exceptions in the Commitment (Exception Documents) other than the standard printed exceptions. Seller authorizes the Title Company to deliver the Commitment and Exception Documents to Buyer at Buyer's address shown in Paragraph 21. If the Commitment and Exception Documents are not delivered to Buyer within the specified time, the time for delivery will be automatically extended up to 15 days or 3 days before the Closing Date, whichever is earlier. If, due to factors beyond Seller's control, the Commitment and Exception Documents are not delivered within the time required, Buyer may terminate this contract and the earnest money will be refunded to Buyer.

C. SURVEY: The survey must be made by a registered professional land surveyor acceptable to the Title Company and Buyer's lender(s). (Check one box only)

☐(1) Within _____ days after the effective date of this contract, Seller shall furnish to Buyer and Title Company Seller's existing survey of the Property and a Residential Real Property Affidavit promulgated by the Texas Department of Insurance (T-47 Affidavit). **If Seller fails to furnish the existing survey or affidavit within the time prescribed, Buyer shall obtain a new survey at Seller's expense no later than 3 days prior to Closing Date.** If the existing survey or affidavit is not acceptable to Title Company or Buyer's lender(s), Buyer shall obtain a new survey at ☐Seller's ☐Buyer's expense no later than 3 days prior to Closing Date.

☐(2) Within _____ days after the effective date of this contract, Buyer shall obtain a new survey at Buyer's expense. Buyer is deemed to receive the survey on the date of actual receipt or the date specified in this paragraph, whichever is earlier.

☐(3) Within _____ days after the effective date of this contract, Seller, at Seller's expense shall furnish a new survey to Buyer.

D. OBJECTIONS: Buyer may object in writing to defects, exceptions, or encumbrances to title: disclosed on the survey other than items 6A(1) through (7) above; disclosed in the Commitment other than items 6A(1) through (8) above; or which prohibit the following use or activity: _____.
Buyer must object the earlier of (i) the Closing Date or (ii) _____ days after Buyer receives the Commitment, Exception Documents, and the survey. Buyer's failure to object within the time allowed will constitute a waiver of Buyer's right to object; except that the requirements in Schedule C of the Commitment are not waived by Buyer. Provided Seller is not obligated to incur any expense, Seller shall cure the timely objections of Buyer or any third party lender within 15 days after Seller receives the objections and the Closing Date will be extended as necessary. If objections are not cured within such 15 day period, this contract will terminate and the earnest money will be refunded to Buyer unless Buyer waives the objections.

E. TITLE NOTICES:

(1) ABSTRACT OR TITLE POLICY: Broker advises Buyer to have an abstract of title covering the Property examined by an attorney of Buyer's selection, or Buyer should be furnished with or obtain a Title Policy. If a Title Policy is furnished, the Commitment should be promptly reviewed by an attorney of Buyer's choice due to the time limitations on Buyer's right to object.

(2) MEMBERSHIP IN PROPERTY OWNERS ASSOCIATION(S): The Property ☐is ☐is not subject to mandatory membership in a property owners association(s). If the Property is subject to mandatory membership in a property owners association(s), Seller notifies Buyer under §5.012, Texas Property Code, that, as a purchaser of property in the residential community identified in Paragraph 2A in which the Property is located, you are obligated to be a member of the property owners association(s). Restrictive covenants governing the use and occupancy of the Property and all dedicatory instruments governing the establishment, maintenance, or operation of this residential community have been or will be recorded in the Real Property Records of the county in which the Property is located. Copies of the restrictive covenants and dedicatory instruments may be obtained from the county clerk. **You are obligated to pay assessments to the property owners association(s). The amount of the assessments is subject to**

The Transaction

Page 2 contains the paragraph that explains how the survey will be handled.
A survey is a drawing of the property boundaries and location of the structures on the land. Your lender will almost certainly require us to obtain a survey.

We will likely ask for the seller to provide a copy of their existing survey to help save you $300-$500 or so. If we are successful at this, I will likely recommend that you obtain a specialized type of insurance to protect you against any errors on that survey by using the paragraph below. This extra insurance is only about $120 on a $380,000 house.

THE TRANSACTION

change. Your failure to pay the assessments could result in enforcement of the association's lien on and the foreclosure of the Property.

Section 207.003, Property Code, entitles an owner to receive copies of any document that governs the establishment, maintenance, or operation of a subdivision, including, but not limited to, restrictions, bylaws, rules and regulations, and a resale certificate from a property owners' association. A resale certificate contains information including, but not limited to, statements specifying the amount and frequency of regular assessments and the style and cause number of lawsuits to which the property owners' association is a party, other than lawsuits relating to unpaid ad valorem taxes of an individual member of the association. These documents must be made available to you by the property owners' association or the association's agent on your request.

If Buyer is concerned about these matters, the TREC promulgated Addendum for Property Subject to Mandatory Membership in a Property Owners Association(s) should be used.

(3) STATUTORY TAX DISTRICTS: If the Property is situated in a utility or other statutorily created district providing water, sewer, drainage, or flood control facilities and services, Chapter 49, Texas Water Code, requires Seller to deliver and Buyer to sign the statutory notice relating to the tax rate, bonded indebtedness, or standby fee of the district prior to final execution of this contract.

(4) TIDE WATERS: If the Property abuts the tidally influenced waters of the state, §33.135, Texas Natural Resources Code, requires a notice regarding coastal area property to be included in the contract. An addendum containing the notice promulgated by TREC or required by the parties must be used.

(5) ANNEXATION: If the Property is located outside the limits of a municipality, Seller notifies Buyer under §5.011, Texas Property Code, that the Property may now or later be included in the extraterritorial jurisdiction of a municipality and may now or later be subject to annexation by the municipality. Each municipality maintains a map that depicts its boundaries and extraterritorial jurisdiction. To determine if the Property is located within a municipality's extraterritorial jurisdiction or is likely to be located within a municipality's extraterritorial jurisdiction, contact all municipalities located in the general proximity of the Property for further information.

(6) PROPERTY LOCATED IN A CERTIFICATED SERVICE AREA OF A UTILITY SERVICE PROVIDER: Notice required by §13.257, Water Code: The real property, described in Paragraph 2, that you are about to purchase may be located in a certificated water or sewer service area, which is authorized by law to provide water or sewer service to the properties in the certificated area. If your property is located in a certificated area there may be special costs or charges that you will be required to pay before you can receive water or sewer service. There may be a period required to construct lines or other facilities necessary to provide water or sewer service to your property. You are advised to determine if the property is in a certificated area and contact the utility service provider to determine the cost that you will be required to pay and the period, if any, that is required to provide water or sewer service to your property. The undersigned Buyer hereby acknowledges receipt of the foregoing notice at or before the execution of a binding contract for the purchase of the real property described in Paragraph 2 or at closing of purchase of the real property.

(7) PUBLIC IMPROVEMENT DISTRICTS: If the Property is in a public improvement district, §5.014, Property Code, requires Seller to notify Buyer as follows: As a purchaser of this parcel of real property you are obligated to pay an assessment to a municipality or county for an improvement project undertaken by a public improvement district under Chapter 372, Local Government Code. The assessment may be due annually or in periodic installments. More information concerning the amount of the assessment and the due dates of that assessment may be obtained from the municipality or county levying the assessment. The amount of the assessments is subject to change. Your failure to pay the assessments could result in a lien on and the foreclosure of your property.

(8) TRANSFER FEES: If the Property is subject to a private transfer fee obligation, §5.205, Property Code, requires Seller to notify Buyer as follows: The private transfer fee obligation may be governed by Chapter 5, Subchapter G of the Texas Property Code.

(9) PROPANE GAS SYSTEM SERVICE AREA: If the Property is located in a propane gas system service area owned by a distribution system retailer, Seller must give Buyer written notice as required by §141.010, Texas Utilities Code. An addendum containing the notice approved by TREC or required by the parties should be used.

(10) NOTICE OF WATER LEVEL FLUCTUATIONS: If the Property adjoins an impoundment of water, including a reservoir or lake, constructed and maintained under Chapter 11, Water Code, that has a storage capacity of at least 5,000 acre-feet at the impoundment's normal operating level, Seller hereby notifies Buyer: "The water level of the impoundment of water adjoining the Property fluctuates for various reasons, including as

THE TRANSACTION

Page 3 of is a continuation of noticies that will only apply to properties in unique situations. For example, purchasers of waterfront property are notified that fluctuation in water levels due to drought or heavy rains could affect the amount of usable property they are purchasing.

THE TRANSACTION

a result of: (1) an entity lawfully exercising its right to use the water stored in the impoundment; or (2) drought or flood conditions."

7.PROPERTY CONDITION:

A. ACCESS, INSPECTIONS AND UTILITIES: Seller shall permit Buyer and Buyer's agents access to the Property at reasonable times. Buyer may have the Property inspected by inspectors selected by Buyer and licensed by TREC or otherwise permitted by law to make inspections. Any hydrostatic testing must be separately authorized by Seller in writing. Seller at Seller's expense shall immediately cause existing utilities to be turned on and shall keep the utilities on during the time this contract is in effect.

B. SELLER'S DISCLOSURE NOTICE PURSUANT TO §5.008, TEXAS PROPERTY CODE (Notice): (Check one box only)

☐ (1) Buyer has received the Notice.

☐ (2) Buyer has not received the Notice. Within _____ days after the effective date of this contract, Seller shall deliver the Notice to Buyer. If Buyer does not receive the Notice, Buyer may terminate this contract at any time prior to the closing and the earnest money will be refunded to Buyer. If Seller delivers the Notice, Buyer may terminate this contract for any reason within 7 days after Buyer receives the Notice or prior to the closing, whichever first occurs, and the earnest money will be refunded to Buyer.

☐ (3)The Seller is not required to furnish the notice under the Texas Property Code.

C. SELLER'S DISCLOSURE OF LEAD-BASED PAINT AND LEAD-BASED PAINT HAZARDS is required by Federal law for a residential dwelling constructed prior to 1978.

D. ACCEPTANCE OF PROPERTY CONDITION: "As Is" means the present condition of the Property with any and all defects and without warranty except for the warranties of title and the warranties in this contract. Buyer's agreement to accept the Property As Is under Paragraph 7D(1) or (2) does not preclude Buyer from inspecting the Property under Paragraph 7A, from negotiating repairs or treatments in a subsequent amendment, or from terminating this contract during the Option Period, if any. (Check one box only)

☐ (1) Buyer accepts the Property As Is.

☐ (2) Buyer accepts the Property As Is provided Seller, at Seller's expense, shall complete the following specific repairs and treatments: _____
_____.
(Do not insert general phrases, such as "subject to inspections" that do not identify specific repairs and treatments.)

E. LENDER REQUIRED REPAIRS AND TREATMENTS: Unless otherwise agreed in writing, neither party is obligated to pay for lender required repairs, which includes treatment for wood destroying insects. If the parties do not agree to pay for the lender required repairs or treatments, this contract will terminate and the earnest money will be refunded to Buyer. If the cost of lender required repairs and treatments exceeds 5% of the Sales Price, Buyer may terminate this contract and the earnest money will be refunded to Buyer.

F. COMPLETION OF REPAIRS AND TREATMENTS: Unless otherwise agreed in writing: (i) Seller shall complete all agreed repairs and treatments prior to the Closing Date; and (ii) all required permits must be obtained, and repairs and treatments must be performed by persons who are licensed to provide such repairs or treatments or, if no license is required by law, are commercially engaged in the trade of providing such repairs or treatments. At Buyer's election, any transferable warranties received by Seller with respect to the repairs and treatments will be transferred to Buyer at Buyer's expense. If Seller fails to complete any agreed repairs and treatments prior to the Closing Date, Buyer may exercise remedies under Paragraph 15 or extend the Closing Date up to 5 days if necessary for Seller to complete the repairs and treatments.

G. ENVIRONMENTAL MATTERS: Buyer is advised that the presence of wetlands, toxic substances, including asbestos and wastes or other environmental hazards, or the presence of a threatened or endangered species or its habitat may affect Buyer's intended use of the Property. If Buyer is concerned about these matters, an addendum promulgated by TREC or required by the parties should be used.

H. RESIDENTIAL SERVICE CONTRACTS: Buyer may purchase a residential service contract from a residential service company licensed by TREC. If Buyer purchases a residential service contract, Seller shall reimburse Buyer at closing for the cost of the residential service contract in an amount not exceeding $_____. Buyer should review any residential service contract for the scope of coverage, exclusions and limitations. **The purchase of a residential service contract is optional. Similar coverage may be purchased from various companies authorized to do business in Texas.**

8.BROKERS' FEES: All obligations of the parties for payment of brokers' fees are contained in separate written agreements.

THE TRANSACTION

We use this paragraph to ask the seller to purchase a Residential Service Contract (aka home warranty) for you. I like to **think of this like extra insurance**. It provides **peace of mind** by protecting you against unexpected repairs shortly after you move. It usually covers items such as the appliances, hot water heater, hvac, or garage door openers. Just like insurance, they have very specific things that they cover and do not cover.

The amount we get the seller to pay is similar to a premium. If an item breaks, you call the company and pay a small deductible, usually $60-$80, for a service technician to come out and fix the item or replace it, if its covered.

THE TRANSACTION

9. CLOSING:

A. The closing of the sale will be on or before _____, 20____, or within 7 days after objections made under Paragraph 6D have been cured or waived, whichever date is later (Closing Date). If either party fails to close the sale by the Closing Date, the non-defaulting party may exercise the remedies contained in Paragraph 15.

B. At closing:

(1) Seller shall execute and deliver a general warranty deed conveying title to the Property to Buyer and showing no additional exceptions to those permitted in Paragraph 6 and furnish tax statements or certificates showing no delinquent taxes on the Property.

(2) Buyer shall pay the Sales Price in good funds acceptable to the escrow agent.

(3) Seller and Buyer shall execute and deliver any notices, statements, certificates, affidavits, releases, loan documents and other documents reasonably required for the closing of the sale and the issuance of the Title Policy.

(4) There will be no liens, assessments, or security interests against the Property which will not be satisfied out of the sales proceeds unless securing the payment of any loans assumed by Buyer and assumed loans will not be in default.

(5) If the Property is subject to a residential lease, Seller shall transfer security deposits (as defined under §92.102, Property Code), if any, to Buyer. In such an event, Buyer shall deliver to the tenant a signed statement acknowledging that the Buyer has acquired the Property and is responsible for the return of the security deposit, and specifying the exact dollar amount of the security deposit.

10. POSSESSION:

A. Buyer's Possession: Seller shall deliver to Buyer possession of the Property in its present or required condition, ordinary wear and tear excepted: ☐ upon closing and funding ☐ according to a temporary residential lease form promulgated by TREC or other written lease required by the parties. Any possession by Buyer prior to closing or by Seller after closing which is not authorized by a written lease will establish a tenancy at sufferance relationship between the parties. **Consult your insurance agent prior to change of ownership and possession because insurance coverage may be limited or terminated. The absence of a written lease or appropriate insurance coverage may expose the parties to economic loss.**

B. Leases:

(1) After the Effective Date, Seller may not execute any lease (including but not limited to mineral leases) or convey any interest in the Property without Buyer's written consent.

(2) If the Property is subject to any lease to which Seller is a party, Seller shall deliver to Buyer copies of the lease(s) and any move-in condition form signed by the tenant within 7 days after the Effective Date of the contract.

11. SPECIAL PROVISIONS:
(Insert only factual statements and business details applicable to the sale. TREC rules prohibit license holders from adding factual statements or business details for which a contract addendum, lease or other form has been promulgated by TREC for mandatory use.)

12. SETTLEMENT AND OTHER EXPENSES:

A. The following expenses must be paid at or prior to closing:

(1) Expenses payable by Seller (Seller's Expenses):

(a) Releases of existing liens, including prepayment penalties and recording fees; release of Seller's loan liability; tax statements or certificates; preparation of deed; one-half of escrow fee; and other expenses payable by Seller under this contract.

(b) Seller shall also pay an amount not to exceed $_____ to be applied in the following order: Buyer's Expenses which Buyer is prohibited from paying by FHA, VA, Texas Veterans Land Board or other governmental loan programs, and then to other Buyer's Expenses as allowed by the lender.

(2) Expenses payable by Buyer (Buyer's Expenses): Appraisal fees; loan application fees; origination charges; credit reports; preparation of loan documents; interest on the notes from date of disbursement to one month prior to dates of first monthly payments; recording fees; copies of easements and restrictions; loan title policy with endorsements required by lender; loan-related inspection fees; photos; amortization schedules; one-half of escrow fee; all prepaid items, including required premiums for flood and hazard insurance, reserve deposits for insurance, ad valorem taxes and special governmental assessments; final compliance inspection; courier fee; repair inspection; underwriting fee; wire transfer fee; expenses incident to any loan; Private

The Transaction

Paragraph 9 is where we will enter the closing deadline. Most transactions take **30-45 days** from beginning to end and end up actually closing within a couple days of the deadline date in this paragraph.

Closing is the meeting where you go sign all the final papers. It usually takes place at the title company. Most closings have only about **4 really important documents**, however depending on the type of financing you get, **there could literally be hundreds** of documents for you to sign. The title company will block off about 1 hour. **This isn't enough time for you to read the documents**. Part of our job will be to recognize if any document looks out of place. If there is a document we believe you shouldn't sign we will stop closing, call the lender or whoever we need to, get to the bottom of the issue, and only proceed once all questions have been resolved. If you would like to read any documents in depth before closing, please discuss this with your lender and let me know so I can help make sure you get all your questions answered and access to the documents in advance.

Paragraph 10 describes when you actually take ownership and possession of the property. This is a **separate event from closing**. After you and the seller sign all the documents at closing, the title company will tell your lender that the closing is complete. Next your lender will authorize the title company to send your loan proceeds to the seller and appropriate locations.
After this happens, its time to celebrate. You can get your keys and begin moving into your new home!

THE TRANSACTION

Mortgage Insurance Premium (PMI), VA Loan Funding Fee, or FHA Mortgage Insurance Premium (MIP) as required by the lender; and other expenses payable by Buyer under this contract.

B. If any expense exceeds an amount expressly stated in this contract for such expense to be paid by a party, that party may terminate this contract unless the other party agrees to pay such excess. Buyer may not pay charges and fees expressly prohibited by FHA, VA, Texas Veterans Land Board or other governmental loan program regulations.

13. **PRORATIONS:** Taxes for the current year, interest, maintenance fees, assessments, dues and rents will be prorated through the Closing Date. The tax proration may be calculated taking into consideration any change in exemptions that will affect the current year's taxes. If taxes for the current year vary from the amount prorated at closing, the parties shall adjust the prorations when tax statements for the current year are available. If taxes are not paid at or prior to closing, Buyer shall pay taxes for the current year.

14. **CASUALTY LOSS:** If any part of the Property is damaged or destroyed by fire or other casualty after the effective date of this contract, Seller shall restore the Property to its previous condition as soon as reasonably possible, but in any event by the Closing Date. If Seller fails to do so due to factors beyond Seller's control, Buyer may (a) terminate this contract and the earnest money will be refunded to Buyer (b) extend the time for performance up to 15 days and the Closing Date will be extended as necessary or (c) accept the Property in its damaged condition with an assignment of insurance proceeds, if permitted by Seller's insurance carrier, and receive credit from Seller at closing in the amount of the deductible under the insurance policy. Seller's obligations under this paragraph are independent of any other obligations of Seller under this contract.

15. **DEFAULT:** If Buyer fails to comply with this contract, Buyer will be in default, and Seller may (a) enforce specific performance, seek such other relief as may be provided by law, or both, or (b) terminate this contract and receive the earnest money as liquidated damages, thereby releasing both parties from this contract. If Seller fails to comply with this contract, Seller will be in default and Buyer may (a) enforce specific performance, seek such other relief as may be provided by law, or both, or (b) terminate this contract and receive the earnest money, thereby releasing both parties from this contract.

16. **MEDIATION:** It is the policy of the State of Texas to encourage resolution of disputes through alternative dispute resolution procedures such as mediation. Any dispute between Seller and Buyer related to this contract which is not resolved through informal discussion will be submitted to a mutually acceptable mediation service or provider. The parties to the mediation shall bear the mediation costs equally. This paragraph does not preclude a party from seeking equitable relief from a court of competent jurisdiction.

17. **ATTORNEY'S FEES:** A Buyer, Seller, Listing Broker, Other Broker, or escrow agent who prevails in any legal proceeding related to this contract is entitled to recover reasonable attorney's fees and all costs of such proceeding.

18. **ESCROW:**
   A. ESCROW: The escrow agent is not (i) a party to this contract and does not have liability for the performance or nonperformance of any party to this contract, (ii) liable for interest on the earnest money and (iii) liable for the loss of any earnest money caused by the failure of any financial institution in which the earnest money has been deposited unless the financial institution is acting as escrow agent.
   B. EXPENSES: At closing, the earnest money must be applied first to any cash down payment, then to Buyer's Expenses and any excess refunded to Buyer. If no closing occurs, escrow agent may: (i) require a written release of liability of the escrow agent from all parties, (ii) require payment of unpaid expenses incurred on behalf of a party, and (iii) only deduct from the earnest money the amount of unpaid expenses incurred on behalf of the party receiving the earnest money.
   C. DEMAND: Upon termination of this contract, either party or the escrow agent may send a release of earnest money to each party and the parties shall execute counterparts of the release and deliver same to the escrow agent. If either party fails to execute the release, either party may make a written demand to the escrow agent for the earnest money. If only one party makes written demand for the earnest money, escrow agent shall promptly provide a copy of the demand to the other party. If escrow agent does not receive written objection to the demand from the other party within 15 days, escrow agent may disburse the earnest money to the party making demand reduced by the amount of unpaid expenses incurred on behalf of the party receiving the earnest money and escrow agent may pay the same to the creditors. If escrow agent complies with the provisions of this paragraph, each party hereby releases escrow agent from all adverse claims related to the disbursal of the earnest money.

THE TRANSACTION

Page 6 explains items that are standard in every real estate transaction. For example, property taxes are prorated. The seller pays all the taxes for the time the seller owns the property and buyer pays for the time the buyer owns the property.

THE TRANSACTION

D. DAMAGES: Any party who wrongfully fails or refuses to sign a release acceptable to the escrow agent within 7 days of receipt of the request will be liable to the other party for (i) damages; (ii) the earnest money; (iii) reasonable attorney's fees; and (iv) all costs of suit.

E. NOTICES: Escrow agent's notices will be effective when sent in compliance with Paragraph 21. Notice of objection to the demand will be deemed effective upon receipt by escrow agent.

19. **REPRESENTATIONS:** All covenants, representations and warranties in this contract survive closing. If any representation of Seller in this contract is untrue on the Closing Date, Seller will be in default. Unless expressly prohibited by written agreement, Seller may continue to show the Property and receive, negotiate and accept back up offers.

20. **FEDERAL TAX REQUIREMENTS:** If Seller is a "foreign person," as defined by applicable law, or if Seller fails to deliver an affidavit to Buyer that Seller is not a "foreign person," then Buyer shall withhold from the sales proceeds an amount sufficient to comply with applicable tax law and deliver the same to the Internal Revenue Service together with appropriate tax forms. Internal Revenue Service regulations require filing written reports if currency in excess of specified amounts is received in the transaction.

21. **NOTICES:** All notices from one party to the other must be in writing and are effective when mailed to, hand-delivered at, or transmitted by fax or electronic transmission as follows:

To Buyer at: _____	**To Seller at:** _____
_____	_____
Phone: ( ) _____	Phone: ( ) _____
Fax: ( ) _____	Fax: ( ) _____
E-mail: _____	E-mail: _____

22. **AGREEMENT OF PARTIES:** This contract contains the entire agreement of the parties and cannot be changed except by their written agreement. Addenda which are a part of this contract are (Check all applicable boxes):

☐ Third Party Financing Addendum

☐ Seller Financing Addendum

☐ Addendum for Property Subject to Mandatory Membership in a Property Owners Association

☐ Buyer's Temporary Residential Lease

☐ Loan Assumption Addendum

☐ Addendum for Sale of Other Property by Buyer

☐ Addendum for Reservation of Oil, Gas and Other Minerals

☐ Addendum for "Back-Up" Contract

☐ Addendum for Coastal Area Property

☐ Environmental Assessment, Threatened or Endangered Species and Wetlands Addendum

☐ Seller's Temporary Residential Lease

☐ Short Sale Addendum

☐ Addendum for Property Located Seaward of the Gulf Intracoastal Waterway

☐ Addendum for Seller's Disclosure of Information on Lead-based Paint and Lead-based Paint Hazards as Required by Federal Law

☐ Addendum for Property in a Propane Gas System Service Area

☐ Other (list): _____

THE TRANSACTION

Page 7 covers more standard items. We will input your contact information in paragraph 21 to ensure you receive all important notices throughout the course of the transaction. This is also the page where we check the boxes of any addendums that will accompany the contract.

THE TRANSACTION

23. TERMINATION OPTION: For nominal consideration, the receipt of which is hereby acknowledged by Seller, and Buyer's agreement to pay Seller $_____ (Option Fee) within 3 days after the effective date of this contract, Seller grants Buyer the unrestricted right to terminate this contract by giving notice of termination to Seller within _____ days after the effective date of this contract (Option Period). Notices under this paragraph must be given by 5:00 p.m. (local time where the Property is located) by the date specified. If no dollar amount is stated as the Option Fee or if Buyer fails to pay the Option Fee to Seller within the time prescribed, this paragraph will not be a part of this contract and Buyer shall not have the unrestricted right to terminate this contract. If Buyer gives notice of termination within the time prescribed, the Option Fee will not be refunded; however, any earnest money will be refunded to Buyer. The Option Fee ☐will ☐will not be credited to the Sales Price at closing. **Time is of the essence for this paragraph and strict compliance with the time for performance is required.**

24. CONSULT AN ATTORNEY BEFORE SIGNING: TREC rules prohibit real estate license holders from giving legal advice. READ THIS CONTRACT CAREFULLY.

Buyer's
Attorney is: _____

Seller's
Attorney is: _____

_____

_____

Phone: ( ) _____

Phone: ( ) _____

Fax: ( ) _____

Fax: ( ) _____

E-mail: _____

E-mail: _____

EXECUTED the _____day of _____, 20_____ (EFFECTIVE DATE).
(BROKER: FILL IN THE DATE OF FINAL ACCEPTANCE.)

_____
Buyer

_____
Seller

_____
Buyer

_____
Seller

THE TRANSACTION

Paragraph 23 is our favorite paragraph of the entire contract.

- This is what will give you the comfort to move forward on placing an offer on a home even if you aren't 100% sure this is the house you want to buy.
- This will pull the property off the market and protect your position to ensure no other buyers can buy the home.

To activate this paragraph, you offer the seller a small fee (approximately $300 on a $300,000 house or 1/10 of 1%) for the option to terminate the contract within a certain amount of time, usually 7 days or so.

- The more money you put down and the less time you allow, the more serious your offer will appear to the seller.
- If you decide to terminate the contract during this period, you will get a full refund of your earnest money.

You only lose your option fee if you back out of the contract. We will write the contract so that any money you offer the seller will be credited to you at closing as long as you go through with the deal.

Securing your position on a $300,000 asset for only $300 offers you incredible leverage during negotiations.

THE TRANSACTION

BROKER INFORMATION
(Print name(s) only. Do not sign)

Other Broker Firm   License No.   Listing Broker Firm   License No.

represents ☐ Buyer only as Buyer's agent   represents ☐ Seller and Buyer as an intermediary
     ☐ Seller as Listing Broker's subagent   ☐ Seller only as Seller's agent

Associate's Name   License No.   Listing Associate's Name   License No.

Licensed Supervisor of Associate License No. Licensed Supervisor of Listing Associate License No.

Other Broker's Address   Fax   Listing Broker's Office Address   Fax

City   State   Zip   City   State   Zip

Associate's Email Address   Phone   Listing Associate's Email Address   Phone

                Selling Associate's Name   License No.

                Licensed Supervisor of Selling Associate License No.

                Selling Associate's Office Address   Fax

                City   State   Zip

                Selling Associate's Email Address   Phone

Listing Broker has agreed to pay Other Broker_____ of the total sales price when the Listing Broker's fee is received. Escrow agent is authorized and directed to pay other Broker from Listing Broker's fee at closing.

OPTION FEE RECEIPT

Receipt of $_____ (Option Fee) in the form of _____ is acknowledged.

_____ _____
Seller or Listing Broker   Date

CONTRACT AND EARNEST MONEY RECEIPT

Receipt of ☐Contract and ☐$_____Earnest Money in the form of _____ is acknowledged.

Escrow Agent: _____ Date: _____

By: _____
           Email Address
_____ Phone: (____)_____
Address
_____ Fax: (____)_____
City   State   Zip

THE TRANSACTION

Page 9 is where we'll list the contact information of any Realtors involved. It also serves as a receipt page for the earnest and option money.

THE TRANSACTION
ACCEPTANCE TO FUNDING

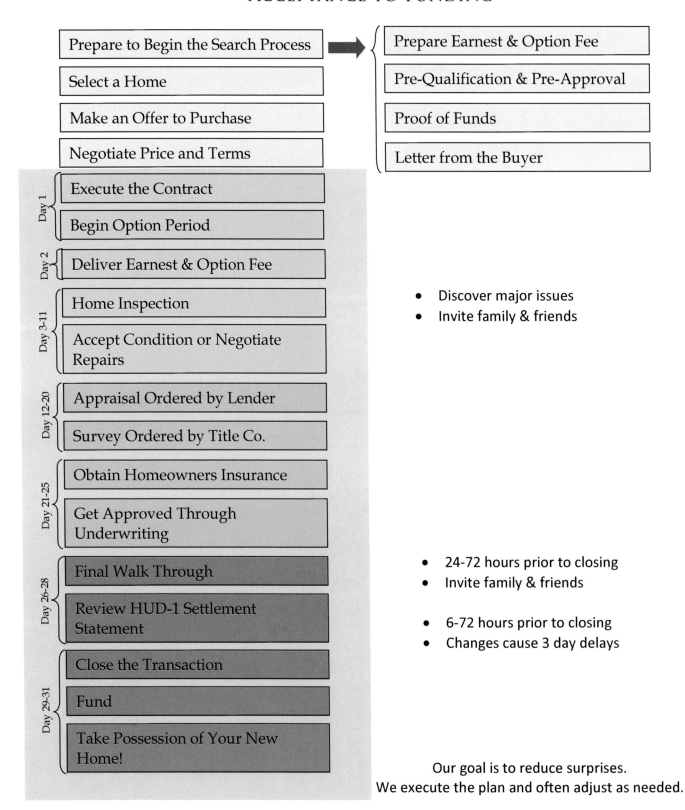

Prepare to Begin the Search Process →

Prepare Earnest & Option Fee

Select a Home

Pre-Qualification & Pre-Approval

Make an Offer to Purchase

Proof of Funds

Negotiate Price and Terms

Letter from the Buyer

Day 1
Execute the Contract

Begin Option Period

Day 2
Deliver Earnest & Option Fee

Day 3-11
Home Inspection

Accept Condition or Negotiate Repairs

- Discover major issues
- Invite family & friends

Day 12-20
Appraisal Ordered by Lender

Survey Ordered by Title Co.

Day 21-25
Obtain Homeowners Insurance

Get Approved Through Underwriting

Day 26-28
Final Walk Through

Review HUD-1 Settlement Statement

- 24-72 hours prior to closing
- Invite family & friends

- 6-72 hours prior to closing
- Changes cause 3 day delays

Day 29-31
Close the Transaction

Fund

Take Possession of Your New Home!

Our goal is to reduce surprises.
We execute the plan and often adjust as needed.

CLIENT REVIEWS

"One of the great real estate companies out there. If you want someone with hands on, valuable business insight in the real estate market then Chandler Crouch is the man for you. He makes the process easier, not harder. As another Broker, I wish there were more people in the real estate business like Chandler Crouch."

- Aimee H., Fort Worth

"I searched forever on my own and couldn't find a house. Then I talked with Chandler and he actually found someone who didn't even have their house on the market. He contacted the seller, helped them work out a short sale with their lender, then we got the deal. It was below market value. When we sold a couple years later I made a nice profit."

- Jonathan P., Fort Worth

"I attended a free home-buying seminar hosted by Chandler Crouch. The seminar was very informative and entertaining. I liked the presenter (Chandler) and the topics covered. I would definitely consider Chandler as my agent on either buy or sell side."

- Nikolay B., Fort Worth

"Chandler is an unbelievable real estate agent! He is an incredible wealth of knowledge and someone that I looked to as a true expert in the real estate industry!"

- Michael S., Fort Worth

"The office is very clean and welcoming. The staff is very friendly and knowledgeable--they will go above and beyond to help in any way possible."

- Drew K., Fort Worth

"We were first time homebuyers and Chandler walked us though every step of the way! He answered every question with kindness and knowledge, insuring that we understood each part of the process. He went to bat for us when negotiating, talking with lenders and even closing personnel to make sure it was all smooth for us. While he offered his advice, he was also careful to ensure we made the best decisions for us and there was never any sort of pressure. Chandler is very knowledgeable about the housing market throughout the entire DFW Metroplex and has advice for various individual neighborhoods as well."

- Tessa R., N. Richland Hills

"Chandler was very helpful from start to finish. Overall customer service was superb. He made

the sale of my house less stressful. He answered every question I had promptly and fully with complete satisfaction. All documents required to be signed were sent quickly and all information was correct."

- Tony S., Fort Worth

"Chandler was an excellent resource in handling my real estate transaction. Residing in Florida was very challenging in scheduling repairs and scheduling utility services for my property; Chandler provided support in these areas over and beyond what would be expected from a realtor. Chandler handled property transactions with various individuals during my absence as a result of living in another state and cared for the property just as he would his own. He also negotiated a selling price close to my listed price. I am happy to recommend him to associates, family and friends in the DFW metroplex. You are in good hands with Chandler!!!"

- Reginald W., Florida

"Chandler Crouch was very professional and knowledgeable with the sale of my house. He guided me through all the steps thru closing and made the process quick and easy. I wouldn't hesitate to recommend Chandler Crouch."

- Cindia F., Fort Worth

"Chandler sold me my first house and has helped pretty much everybody in my family with their real estate needs since about 2003. I trust him. It also doesn't hurt that everybody I know that has bought a house through him has made a nice profit. You're making a mistake if you use anyone else."

- Nathan M., Grand Prairie

"Chandler is THE go to guy. Chandler is an extraordinary person who is able to see the good in every situation, in life and in work. With his positive disposition, he has the ability to inspire those around him no matter the circumstances they are in. During the time I met Chandler, I was in a difficult position in my personal life and needed help with my home. Chandler went out of his way to help me get through this time. He went above and beyond anything I've ever known anyone to do for a client. Chandler is always in an upbeat mood, he always answers his phone and never misses a beat. There is no one else I would rather work with."

- Cindy M., Little Elm

"Chandler helped us find a rental when we were in the process of moving from Hawaii to Texas.

He gave us options that accommodated to our needs and we were able to set up the rental in time for quick move in once we arrived in Texas. We look forward to working with him when we decide to purchase here."

- Raelene P., Fort Worth

"I was very impressed by Chandler and his entire team, the staff was professional and they really knew their stuff. I looked for a house on my own for months and it became overwhelming because it took up too much of my time, a friend recommended I call Chandler and I'm glad I did. After looking for only a couple weeks with Chandler I found the perfect house for me and my family. Chandler was not only professional and really knowledgeable but he was available whenever I needed him. I would recommend this group to any of my friends and family."

- Gina S., Lewisville

"I bought my house through Chandler & his team. I interviewed 7 Realtors (I'm pretty particular), nobody came close to Chandler. He actually answered his phone and had high level advice. This guy knows strategy and negotiation unlike any other Realtor I've dealt with. The seller didn't take our offer at first because it wasn't the highest offer, but then he negotiated and got them to take the offer. We would have lost the house with any other agent. His team agent, Steve, was who showed us houses. He knows the market inside and out. I've sent him referrals from everybody I know... never heard a complaint. When I need to sell, I already know who I'm calling."

- Jeff W., Lewisville

" I was in between jobs. One day I saw a posting on Craigslist for Property Support Specialist. At first it look like some scam. But I went to seminar and it turned out to be a great opportunity for me. Chandler is great guy to work with. I learnt lot of things about Real Estate. I enjoyed working for him. Chandler is very dedicated and knowledgeable Realtor I have ever seen. His seminars are always informative. I would highly recommend attending one of his seminar if you are thinking to buy new house in near future."

- Krupal P., Fort Worth

"My experience with Chandler Crouch Realtors has been truly amazing. I highly recommend Chandler Crouch for your next broker. He has been recommended and followed by a huge number of professionals in Texas, be it realtors or agents. I personally thank him for his business. I wish to tell the world how awesome to do business with him and the rest of the team. I know I won't regret recommending him to everyone."

- CJ M., Fort Worth

"I have worked many transactions with Chandler Crouch and his team. On every occasion, they

went beyond what they had to, to facilitate a smooth process. I've worked with many HUD agents in the DFW area, and none provide the level of professionalism in term of communication, support and education that Chandler Crouch and his team exhibit."

- Beau H., Dallas

"Chandler was wonderful to work with—the financing on the property became and issue and he was on the phone with me helping figure out a solution. I truly appreciated his help. In general, just a great guy!"

- Lisa M., Trophy Club

Reference contact information is available upon request.

OUR FEES

Our Services Are Completely FREE to You.

But not only that, we don't earn any compensation for our work until your goals have been accomplished. You don't pay a dime because we negotiate for the seller to pay our fee at closing.

Until closing, all of the work we do is an investment to help you achieve your goals. Our dedication to you is based on our commitment to provide the highest quality service and to strive for the best possible outcome in meeting your real estate goals.
The only thing we ask for in return is your **loyalty.**

Are you ready to put me to work for you?

To take the next step in achieving your real estate goals, please contact our office to receive a free no commitment consultation by contacting us at:

Ph: 817-381-3800
hello@chandlercrouch.com

TAKING NOTES ON HOMES YOU SEE

Home #1

Address _____

Price _____Style_____Sqft_____

Comments (negative) _____

_____

_____

Comments (positive) _____

_____

_____

Home #2

Address _____

Price _____Style_____Sqft_____

Comments (negative) _____

_____

_____

Comments (positive) _____

_____

_____

Home #3

Address _____

Price _____Style_____Sqft_____

Comments (negative) _____

_____

_____

Comments (positive) _____

_____

_____

Home #4

Address _____

Price _____Style_____Sqft_____

Comments (negative) _____

_____

_____

Comments (positive) _____

_____

_____

Home #5

Address _____

Price _____Style_____Sqft_____

Comments (negative) _____

_____

_____

Comments (positive) _____

_____

_____

Home #6

Address _____

Price _____Style_____Sqft_____

Comments (negative) _____

_____

_____

Comments (positive) _____

_____

_____

DREAM HOME SUCCESS SCHEDULE

Let's stick to this plan to successfully secure your dream home!

A successful real estate transaction hinges on numerous details involving deadlines that must be met so that you can move into your dream home as soon as possible.

Seller's disclosure needs to be filled out and signed by: _____

Schedule the inspection to be completed by: _____

Inspection completed by: _____

Written notice due – all major items from inspection
that you would like the seller to address: _____

Negotiation of inspection complete: _____

Appraisal due by:
Homeowners insurance due by: _____

Buyer's financing must be approved by: _____

Closing deadline: _____

Made in the USA
Monee, IL
17 February 2021